Crossword Poems

Volume One

Crossword Poems

An Anthology of a different kind

Volume One

Ᵽ

PARSIMONY PRESS
2000

There are a number of living people who made it possible to bring these books into print. But the real dedication should be to the people whose verse is included, and to those whose verse should have been included had there been room to do so.

First published in the UK in 2000
Second impression 2000
by Parsimony Press Ltd
West Huntspill, Somerset

Introduction and selection copyright
© Robert Norton, 2000.

ISBN 1 902979 10 9

Typesetting by MacDonald, Miles & Russell Enterprises
Printed and bound by Tien Wah Press, Singapore

It was around the 1950s when schools stopped teaching many of the things that had been part of what every child was exposed to for a great many years. Latin slipped off the curriculum. If there was poetry in the new lessons it tended to become contemporary poetry, much of which lacked the strict rhyme and meter that made learning stuff slightly less of a pain.

In those days the cryptic crosswords that appeared in papers like *The Times* were loaded with allusions that it was expected everybody would recognise. 'Let the dog see the rabbit' was the compiler's motto, and it was rare not to have a quotation with a missing word which gave the solver a start. The number of people who could quote more than four lines of Byron's poem *The Destruction of Sennacherib* would probably have fitted easily into a telephone box. But the number of people who knew the lines *'The Assyrian came down like the wolf on the fold, And his cohorts were gleaming in purple and gold'* might have, with ease, filled all the football stadiums in Britain and still have many to spare.

This book is to remind those who were born before the Hitler War of what they once knew, and to introduce those born after to what their parents and grandparents once knew. The lines in red are those the crossword clues could have drawn from. The rest is what the compilers reasonably assumed had been forgotten. Every now and then there is a loose word in black. That is because when people have been asked to repeat what they remember they have commonly got one word wrong.

The poems are untitled except where one is needed, and are in alphabetical order of the first line.

Known as the Manx poet, he also wrote a much nicer poem than this about a blackbird, in the gathering dark. It is a pity that he is remembered more for this. But with two poems in many of the anthologies, he is doing better than most.

A garden is a lovesome thing, God wot!
    Rose plot,
    Fringed pool,
Fern'd grot—
    The veriest School
    Of peace; and yet the fool
Contends that God is not—
Not God! in gardens! when the eve is cool?
    Nay, but I have a sign;
    'Tis very sure God walks in mine.

Herrick was an unlikely poet, being the seventh child of a prosperous goldsmith. Before he was two years old his father died in a fall from a fourth floor window only two days after making his will. The estate of suicides in those days went to the crown, but the Herricks were given the benefit of the doubt. Robert started life apprenticed to his uncle, also a goldsmith, a knight, and an MP. It was only when he was in his twenties that he went to St John's College Cambridge and started a life that led through BA and MA to priesthood in 1623. There is a gentleness in his poetry that makes it worth re-reading more than once or twice.

A sweet disorder in the dress
Kindles in clothes a wantonness:
A lawn about the shoulders thrown
Into a fine distraction:
An erring lace, which here and there
Enthrals the crimson stomacher:
A cuff neglectful, and thereby
Ribbands to flow confusedly:
A winning wave, deserving note,
In the tempestuous petticoat:
A careless shoe-string, in whose tie
I see a wild civility:
Do more bewitch me than when art
Is too precise in every part.

JOHN KEATS (1795-1821)

Byron called him 'Piss-in-the-bed Keats' perhaps from jealousy that so unadventurous a person should be so highly regarded. Tennyson thought him the best poet of the 19th century. Unlike Herrick he was born into a poorish family, but like Herrick he didn't really begin to write until he had cancelled his apprenticeship to an apothecary-surgeon. He was twenty two when his first volume of poetry appeared. Other books followed, but he struggled with illness and money troubles, and he was only 26 when he died in Italy soon after he had gone there at Shelley's suggestion.

Bards of Passion and of Mirth,
Ye have left your souls on earth!
Have ye souls in heaven too,
Double-lived in regions new?
Yes, and those of heaven commune
With the spheres of sun and moon;
With the noise of fountains wondrous,
And the parle of voices thund'rous;
With the whisper of heaven's trees
And one another, in soft ease
Seated on Elysian lawns
Browsed by none but Dian's fawns;
Underneath large blue-bells tented,
Where the daisies are rose-scented,
And the rose herself has got
Perfume which on earth is not;
Where the nightingale doth sing
Not a senseless, trancèd thing,
But a divine melodious truth;

Philosophic numbers smooth;
Tales and golden histories
Of heaven and its mysteries.

Thus ye live on high, and then
On the earth ye live again;
And the souls ye left behind you
Teach us, here, the way to find you,
Where your other souls are joying,
Never slumber'd, never cloying.
Here, your earth-born souls still speak
To mortals, of their little week;
Of their sorrows and delights;
Of their passions and their spites;
Of their glory and their shame;
What doth strengthen and what maim.
Thus ye teach us, every day,
Wisdom, though fled far away.

Bards of Passion and of Mirth,
Ye have left your souls on earth!
Ye have souls in heaven too,
Double-lived in regions new!

Fair daffodils, we weep to see
    You haste away so soon;
As yet the early-rising sun
    Has not attain'd his noon.
        Stay, stay
    Until the hasting day
        Has run
    But to the evensong;
And, having pray'd together, we
    Will go with you along.

We have short time to stay, as you,
    We have as short a spring;
As quick a growth to meet decay,
    As you, or anything.
        We die
    As your hours do, and dry
        Away
    Like to the summer's rain;
Or as the pearls of morning's dew,
    Ne'er to be found again.

This isn't a poem that many people have read in the last hundred years, although the first line comes up again and again. H E Bates used it as the title of one of his books. But if you want a description of Agincourt, it reads better than one of the Gulf War in The Sun *newspaper. And tells you more, not necessarily with any greater accuracy than you would find in* The Sun. *For the battle was fought in 1415, and Drayton was born in 1563. Drayton lived longer and travelled less than many of the other poets in this collection, but he at least ended up buried in Westminster Abbey.*

Fair stood the wind for France
When we our sails advance,
Nor now to prove our chance
   Longer will tarry;
But putting to the main,
At Caux, the mouth of Seine,
With all his martial train
   Landed King Harry.

And taking many a fort,
Furnish'd in warlike sort,
Marcheth tow'rds Agincourt
   In happy hour;
Skirmishing day by day
With those that stopp'd his way,
Where the French gen'ral lay
   With all his power.

Which, in his height of pride,
King Henry to deride,
His ransom to provide
    Unto him sending;
Which he neglects the while
As from a nation vile,
Yet with an angry smile
    Their fall portending.

And turning to his men,
Quoth our brave Henry then,
'Though they to one be ten
    Be not amazèd:
Yet have we well begun;
Battles so bravely won
Have ever to the sun
    By fame been raisèd.

'And for myself (quoth he)
This my full rest shall be:
England ne'er mourn for me
    Nor more esteem me:
Victor I will remain
Or on this earth lie slain,
Never shall she sustain
    Loss to redeem me.

'Poitiers and Cressy tell,
When most their pride did swell,
Under our swords they fell:
    No less our skill is

Than when our grandsire great,
Claiming the regal seat,
By many a warlike feat
    Lopp'd the French lilies.'

The Duke of York so dread
The eager vaward led;
With the main Henry sped
    Among his henchmen.
Excester had the rear,
A braver man not there;
O Lord, how hot they were
    On the false Frenchmen!

They now to fight are gone,
Armour on armour shone,
Drum now to drum did groan,
    To hear was wonder;
That with the cries they make
The very earth did shake:
Trumpet to trumpet spake,
    Thunder to thunder.

Well it thine age became,
O noble Erpingham,
Which didst the signal aim
    To our hid forces!
When from a meadow by,
Like a storm suddenly
The English archery
    Stuck the French horses.

With Spanish yew so strong,
Arrows a cloth-yard long
That like to serpents stung,
   Piercing the weather;
None from his fellow starts,
But playing manly parts,
And like true English hearts
   Stuck close together.

When down their bows they threw,
And forth their bilbos drew,
And on the French they flew,
   Not one was tardy;
Arms were from shoulders sent,
Scalps to the teeth were rent,
Down the French peasants went—
   Our men were hardy.

This while our noble king,
His broadsword brandishing,
Down the French host did ding
   As to o'erwhelm it;
And many a deep wound lent,
His arms with blood besprent,
And many a cruel dent
   Bruisèd his helmet.

Gloster, that duke so good,
Next of the royal blood,
For famous England stood
   With his brave brother;

Clarence, in steel so bright,
Though but a maiden knight,
Yet in that furious fight
    Scarce such another.

Warwick in blood did wade,
Oxford the foe invade,
And cruel slaughter made
    Still as they ran up;
Suffolk his axe did ply,
Beaumont and Willoughby
Bare them right doughtily,
    Ferrers and Fanhope.

Upon Saint Crispin's Day
Fought was this noble fray,
Which fame did not delay
    To England to carry
O when shall English men
With such acts fill a pen?
Or England breed again
    Such a King Harry?

TO THE VIRGINS, TO MAKE MUCH OF TIME
ROBERT HERRICK

Gather ye rosebuds while ye may,
  Old Time is still a-flying:
And this same flower that smiles to-day
  To-morrow will be dying.

The glorious lamp of heaven, the sun,
  The higher he's a-getting,
The sooner will his race be run,
  And nearer he's to setting.

That age is best which is the first,
  When youth and blood are warmer;
But being spent, the worse, and worst
  Times still succeed the former.

Then be not coy, but use your time,
  And while ye may, go marry:
For having lost but once your prime,
  You may forever tarry.

Few girls with an interest in English literature have been able to escape the attraction of Donne. We show our knowledge by pronouncing his name to rhyme with 'bun'.

Apart from his poems ('Busy old fool, unruly sun', 'Stay, O sweet, and do not rise!', 'Dear love, for nothing less than thee' *and so on) we are also constantly reminded of his* 'Bell sermon' *and the phrases* 'No man is an island' *and* 'Ask not for whom the bell tolls. It tolls for thee.' *Unlike those of many of his contemporaries, all these, his love poems and his essays come in bite-sized chunks and this makes them easier to handle if you are in the least bit tired.*

> Goe and catche a falling starre,
>> Get with child a mandrake roote,
> Tell me, where all past yeares are,
>> Or who cleft the Divels foot;
> Teach me to heare mermaides singing,
> Or to keep off envies stinging,
>> And finde
>> What winde
> Serves to advance an honest minde.
>
> If thou beest borne to strange sights,
>> Things invisible to see,
> Ride ten thousand daies and nights

Till age snow white haires on thee;
Thou, when thou retorn'st, wilt tell mee
All strange wonders that befell thee,
    And sweare
    No where
Lives a woman true, and faire.

If thou findst one, let mee know;
    Such a pilgrimage were sweet.
Yet doe not; I would not goe,
    Though at next doore wee might meet.
Though shee were true when you met her,
And last till you write your letter,
    Yet shee
    Will bee
False, ere I come, to two, or three.

ELIZABETH BARRETT BROWNING
(1806-1861)

This was an extraordinarily well-educated woman, the eldest of twelve children in a family wealthy from their holdings in the West Indies. In her early thirties she became an invalid, and in her thirty-ninth year Robert Browning began a correspondence with her. This, despite her father's forbidding any of his children to marry, led to their meeting. They married the following year and went to Italy, where she stayed until she died, 28 years before her husband at the age of only 55. The beauty of her poems was widely recognised, and at the death of Wordsworth in 1850, there were many who wanted her to be the next Poet Laureate. This, the best known of her Sonnets from the Portuguese, is for many people the best love poem ever written in the English language.

How do I love thee? Let me count the ways.
I love thee to the depth and breadth and height
My soul can reach, when feeling out of sight
For the ends of Being and ideal Grace.
I love thee to the level of every day's
Most quiet need, by sun and candle-light.
I love thee freely, as men strive for Right;
I love thee purely, as they turn from Praise.
I love thee with the passion put to use
In my old griefs, and with my childhood's faith.
I love thee with a love I seemed to lose
With my lost saints,—I love thee with the breath,
Smiles, tears, of all my life!—and, if God choose,
I shall but love thee better after death.

SAMUEL TAYLOR COLERIDGE
(1772-1834)

Ah. Here we have a gem of a poem, by a gem of a man. Here he was, high as a kite, scribbling away, when he was interrupted by a 'person from Porlock'. The poem never got finished, but if you work on the basis that to be told a dream is one of the miseries that we occasionally have to bear, this one is one that is worth listening to.

In Xanadu did Kubla Kahn
    A stately pleasure-dome decree:
Where Alph, the sacred river, ran
Through caverns measureless to man
    Down to a sunless sea.
So twice five miles of fertile ground
    With walls and towers were girdled round:
And there were gardens bright with sinuous rills
Where blossom'd many an incense-bearing tree;
And here were forests ancient as the hills,
Enfolding sunny spots of greenery.

But O, that deep romantic chasm which slanted
Down the green hills athwart a cedarn cover!
A savage place! as holy and enchanted
As e'er beneath a waning moon was haunted
By woman wailing for her demon-lover!
And from this chasm, with ceaseless turmoil seething,
As if this earth in fast thick pants were breathing,
A mighty fountain momently was forced;
Amid whose swift half-intermitted burst
Huge fragments vaulted like rebounding hail,
Or chaffy grain beneath the thresher's flail:

And 'mid these dancing rocks at once and ever
It flung up momently the sacred river.
Five miles meandering with a mazy motion
Through wood and dale the sacred river ran,
Then reach'd the caverns measureless to man,
And sank in tumult to a lifeless ocean:
And 'mid this tumult Kubla heard from far
Ancestral voices prophesying war!
 The shadow of the dome of pleasure
  Floated midway on the waves;
 Where was heard the mingled measure
 From the fountain and the caves
It was a miracle of rare device,
A sunny pleasure-dome with caves of ice!

 A damsel with a dulcimer
  In a vision I once saw:
It was an Abyssinian maid,
  And on her dulcimer she play'd,
Singing of Mount Abora.
 Could I revive within me,
 Her symphony and song,
To such a deep delight 'twould win me,
That with music loud and long,
I would build that dome in air,
That sunny dome! those caves of ice!
And all who heard should see them there,
And all should cry, Beware! Beware!
His flashing eyes, his floating hair!
Weave a circle round him thrice,
 And close your eyes with holy dread,
 For he on honey-dew hath fed,
 And drunk the milk of Paradise.

Like Coleridge and Charles Lamb, Leigh Hunt went to school at Christ's Hospital, but unlike them there was no House named after him when the school moved to Horsham. This may be because he spent two years in gaol when he and his brother were put there for a libel on the Prince Regent. Nevertheless, like Raleigh in the Tower, he was allowed to have his family with him, and he was constantly visited by friends as varied as Keats (whom he introduced to the world in The Examiner*), or Byron, Thomas Moore and Jeremy Bentham.*

He was a prolific writer and was much loved by his contemporaries for his happy nature. He must also have earned gratitude for bringing so much of their early work into print in The Examiner. *As an editor he had a great gift for spotting talent.*

Jenny kiss'd me when we met,
    Jumping from the chair she sat in;
Time, you thief, who love to get
    Sweets into your list, put that in!
Say I'm weary, say I'm sad,
    Say that health and wealth have miss'd me,
Say I'm growing old, but add,
      Jenny kiss'd me.

This is the first anonymous poem. If you elected to fill a book with only beautiful anonymous poems it would be a very thick book.

It is very gratifying to know that even if there is no writer behind it wanting to make it known, it will still be remembered because it is worth remembering.

Love **not me** for comely grace,
For my pleasing eye or face,
Nor for any outward part,
No, nor for a constant heart:
    For these may fail or turn to ill,
    So thou and I shall sever:
Keep, therefore, a true woman's eye,
And love me still but know not why—
    So hast thou the same reason still
    To doat upon me ever!

WALTER SAVAGE LANDOR
(1775-1864)

What is perhaps the most surprising thing about Landor was that he died in 1864 at the age of 89. One would expect that somebody would have seen him off a bit sooner. He started by being kicked out of school for insubordination, and through his life he quarrelled with everybody, including the wife he married in 1811. There is even the story that he once threw the cook out of the ground floor window, and then clapped his hand to his head in remorse. Not for the cook, though. For the flowers on which she landed.

Yet he wrote this.

Mother, I cannot mind my wheel;
    My fingers ache, my lips are dry:
O, if you felt the pain I feel!
    But O, who ever felt as I?

No longer could I doubt him true—
    All other men may use deceit;
He always said my eyes were blue,
    And often swore my lips were sweet.

ON FIRST LOOKING INTO CHAPMAN'S
HOMER
JOHN KEATS

Much have I travell'd in the realms of gold,
And many goodly states and kingdoms seen;
Round many western islands have I been
Which bards in fealty to Apollo hold.
Oft of one wide expanse had I been told
That deep-brow'd Homer ruled as his demesne:
Yet did I never breathe its pure serene
Till I heard Chapman speak out loud and bold:
Then felt I like some watcher of skies
When a new planet swims into his ken;
Or like stout Cortez, when with eagle eyes
He stared at the Pacific—and all his men
    Look'd at each other with a wild surmise—
    Silent, upon a peak in Darien.

No, no! go not to Lethe, neither twist
　　Wolf's-bane, tight-rooted, for its poisonous wine:
Nor suffer thy pale forehead to be kist
　　By nightshade, ruby grape of Proserpine;
Make not your rosary of yew-berries,
　　Nor let the beetle, nor the death-moth be
　　　　Your mournful Psyche, nor the downy owl
A partner in your sorrow's mysteries;
　　For shade to shade will come too drowsily,
　　　　And drown the wakeful anguish of the soul.

But when the melancholy fit shall fall
　　Sudden from heaven like a weeping cloud,
That fosters the droop-headed flowers all,
　　And hides the green hill in an April shroud;
Then glut thy sorrow on a morning rose,
　　Or on the rainbow of the salt sand-wave,
　　　　Or on the wealth of globèd peonies;
Or if thy mistress some rich anger shows,
　　Emprison her soft hand, and let her rave,
　　　　And feed deep, deep upon her peerless eyes

She dwells with Beauty—Beauty that must die;
　　And Joy, whose hand is ever at his lips
Bidding adieu; and aching Pleasure nigh,
　　Turning to poison while the bee-mouth sips:
Ay, in the very temple of Delight
　　Veil'd Melancholy has her sovran shrine,
Though seen of none save him whose strenuous tongue
Can burst Joy's grape against his palate fine;
　　His soul shall taste the sadness of her might,
　　　　And be among her cloudy trophies hung.

More damage than he deserves has been done to the appreciation of Burns by the fuss that the Scots make of him. It is hard enough for non-Scots to handle the dialect without having to put up with the idea that he is slightly more important than the Almighty. We will skip Auld Land Syne, *and we will skip the* 'wee, timourous beestie', *and show him with this poem, which has also since become one of the nicest songs we know. If you do hear it sung, you will probably want to see the words written down so that you can sing it yourself in the bath.*

O Mary, at thy window be,
It is the wish'd, the trysted hour!
Those smiles and glances let me see,
    That make the miser's treasure poor:
How blythely wad I bide the stour
    A weary slave frae sun to sun,
Could I the rich reward secure,
    The lovely Mary Morison!

Yestreen, when to the trembling string
    The dance gaed thro' the lighted ha',
To thee my fancy took its wing,
    I sat, but neither heard nor saw:
Tho' this was fair, and that was braw,
    And yon the toast of a' the town,
I sigh'd and said amang them a',
    'Ye arena Mary Morison.'
O Mary, canst thou wreck his peace,
    Wha for thy sake wad gladly die?

Or canst thou break that heart of his,
  Whase only faut is loving thee?
If love for love thou wiltna gie,
  At least be pity to me shown;
A thought ungentle canna be
  The thought o' Mary Morison.

HOME THOUGHTS FROM ABROAD
ROBERT BROWNING (1812-1889)

The best remembered mark that Browning has made on
the literary world is his courtship of Elizabeth Barrett.
But of all his poems this one is highest on the Crossword
list. We even remember a cartoon in Punch, a little
bespectacled schoolgirl in the countryside surrounded
by what must be a botany class and the teacher. The caption
was 'Oh, look, Miss Jones! Ranunculus bulbosus, the
little children's dower, far brighter than this gaudy
cucumis melo!' *It was clearly understood that, among*
Punch readers at least, no explanation would be necessary.

Oh, to be in England
Now that April's there,
And whoever wakes in England
Sees, some morning, unaware
That the lowest boughs **and** the brushwood sheaf
Round the elm-tree bole are in tiny leaf,
While the chaffinch sings on the orchard bough
In England,—now!

And after April, when May follows,
And the whitethroat builds, and all the swallows—
Hark! Where my blossomed pear-tree in the hedge
Leans to the field and scatters on the clover
Blossoms and dewdrops—at the bent-spray's edge—
That's the wise thrush; he sings each song twice over,
Lest you should think he never could recapture
The first fine careless rapture!

And though the fields look rough with hoary dew,
All will be gay when noontide wakes anew
The buttercups, the little children's dower,
—Far brighter than this gaudy melon-flower!

O what a plague is love!
    How shall I bear it?
She will inconstant prove,
    I greatly fear it.
She so torments my mind
    That my strength faileth,
And wavers with the wind
    As a ship saileth.
Please her the best I may,
She loves still to gainsay;
Alack and well-a-day!
    Phillada flouts me.

At the fair yesterday
    She did pass by me;
She look'd another way
    And would not spy me:
I woo'd her for to dine,
    But could not get her;
Will had her to the wine—
    He might entreat her.
With Daniel she did dance,
On me she look'd askance:
O thrice unhappy chance!
    Phillada flouts me.

Fair maid, be not so coy,
    Do not disdain me!
I am my mother's joy:
    Sweet, entertain me!
She'll give me, when she dies,
    All that is fitting:
Her poultry and her bees,
    And her goose sitting,
A pair of mattrass beds,
And a bag full of shreds;
And yet, for all this guedes,
    Phillada flouts me!

She hath a clout of mine
    Wrought with blue coventry,
Which she keeps for a sign
    Of my fidelity:
But i' faith, if she flinch
    She shall not wear it;
To Tib, my t'other wench,
    I mean to bear it.
And yet it grieves my heart
So soon from her to part:
Death strike me with his dart!
    Phillada flouts me.

Thou shalt eat crudded cream
    All the year lasting,
And drink the crystal stream
    Pleasant in tasting;
Whig and whey whilst thou lust,
    And bramble-berries,
Pie-lid and pastry-crust,
    Pears, plums, and cherries.
Thy raiment shall be thin,
Made of a weevil's skin—
Yet all's not worth a pin!
    Phillada flouts me.

In the last month of May
    I made her posies;
I heard her often say
    That she loves roses.
Cowslips and gillyflowers
    And the white lily
I brought to deck the bowers
    For my sweet Philly.
But she did all disdain,
And threw them back again;
Therefore 'tis flat and plain
    Phillada flouts me.

Fair maiden, have a care,
    And in time take me;
I can have those as fair
    If you forsake me:
For Doll the dairy-maid
    Laugh'd at me lately,
And wanton Winifred
    Favours me greatly.
One throws milk on my clothes,
T'other plays with my nose;
What wanting signs are those?
    Phillada flouts me.

I cannot work nor sleep
    At all in season:
Love wounds my heart so deep
    Without all reason.
I 'gin to pine away
    In my love's shadow,
Like as a fat beast may,
    Penn'd in a meadow.
I shall be dead, I fear,
Within this thousand year:
And all for that my dear
    Phillada flouts me.

guedes = property

35

Carey is a man, born in the 15th century and died in the 16th, who wrote all sorts of things for the theatre that were extremely popular at the time. But he comes down to us only for this poem, and as the man who was the first to call somebody Namby Pamby. This was a poet, Ambrose Philips, who was rash enough to write soppy poems for children, perhaps as an antidote to a long standing feud he had with Alexander Pope.

One of the farces Carey wrote was about a man called Chrononhotonthologos who was king of Queerummania. The names of the characters include the one called Aldiborontiphoscophornia, which so delighted Sir Walter Scott that he used it for a man called James Ballantyne, whom he thought pompous enough to deserve the name. If you can work out how to pronounce these words you may have the use of a good conversation stopper.

Of all the girls that are so smart
There's none like pretty Sally;
She is the darling of my heart,
And she lives in our alley.
There is no lady in the land
Is half so sweet as Sally;
She is the darling of my heart,
And she lives in our alley.

Her father he makes cabbage-nets,
    And through the streets does cry 'em;
Her mother she sells laces long
    To such as please to buy 'em:
But sure such folks could ne'er beget
    So sweet a girl as Sally!
She is the darling of my heart,
    And she lives in our alley.

When she is by, I leave my work,
    I loved her so sincerely;
My master comes like any Turk,
    And bangs me most severely:
But let him bang his bellyful,
    I'll bear it all for Sally;
She is the darling of my heart,
And she lives in our alley.

Of all the days that's in the week
    I dearly love but one day—
And that's the day that comes betwixt
    A Saturday and Monday;
For then I'm drest all in my best
    To walk abroad with Sally;
She is the darling of my heart,
    And she lives in our alley.

My master carries me to church,
    And often am I blamèd
Because I leave him in the lurch
    As soon as text is namèd;
I leave the church in sermon-time
    And slink away to Sally;
She is the darling of my heart,
    And she lives in our alley.

When Christmas comes about again,
    O, then I shall have money;
I'll hoard it up, and box it all,
    I'll give it to my honey:
I would it were ten thousand pound,
    I'd give it all to Sally;
She is the darling of my heart,
    And she lives in our alley.

My master and the neighbours all
    Make game of me and Sally,
And, but for her, I'd better be
    A slave and row a galley;
But when my seven long years are out
    O, then I'll marry Sally;
O, then we'll wed, and then we'll bed—
    But not in our alley!

MATTHEW ARNOLD (1822-88)

Matthew Arnold was the eldest son of Thomas Arnold, who introduced the changes to Rugby School that made him much-loved by his pupils, many of whom, including his son Matthew, became famous.

After Rugby Matthew did extraordinarily well at Oxford, and became a fellow of Oriel. When he was 29 he both married and became an inspector of schools, a job that he held for the next thirty five years. Although he became professor of Poetry at Oxford in his late thirties, he wrote less verse and more prose, most of it critical of many of the current attitudes in education and politics.

Of his poetry, Dover Beach *is what we most remember, but unlike this gentle poem pointing out how little people understood Shakespeare's genius during his lifetime,* Dover Beach *has three lines that merit a place in a crossword clue. This has only one.*

Others abide our question. Thou art free.
We ask and ask: Thou smilest and art still,
Out-topping knowledge. For the loftiest hill
That to the stars uncrowns his majesty,
Planting his steadfast footsteps in the sea,
Making the heaven of heavens his dwelling-place,
Spares but the cloudy border of his base
To the foil'd searching of mortality;
And thou, who didst the stars and sunbeams know,
Self-school'd, self-scann'd, self-honour'd, self-secure,
Didst walk on earth unguess'd at. Better so!

All pains the immortal spirit must endure,
    All weakness that impairs, all griefs that bow,
    Find their sole voice in that victorious brow.

MATIN SONG
THOMAS HEYWOOD (1574-1641)

*Born about ten years after Shakespeare, in the middle of
the 1570s, Heywood wrote well over a hundred plays.
Perhaps* The Fair Maid of the West *is the only title to
survive to this day.*

Students of the theatre also recommend his An
Apology for Actors, *which was published in 1612.*

Pack, clouds, away! and welcome, day!
   With night we banish sorrow,
Sweet air, blow soft; mount, lark, aloft
   To give my Love good-morrow!
Wings from the wind to please her mind,
   Notes from the lark I'll borrow:
Bird, prune thy wing! nightingale, sing!
   To give my Love good-morrow!
   To give my Love good-morrow!
   Notes from them all I'll borrow.

Wake from thy nest, robin red-breast!
   Sing, birds, in every furrow!
And from each bill let music shrill
   Give my fair Love good-morrow!
Blackbird and thrush in every bush,
   Stare, linnet, and cocksparrow,
You pretty elves, among yourselves
   Sing my fair Love good-morrow!
   To give my Love good-morrow!
   Sing, birds, in every furrow!

If you had the chance of living the life of someone from the past you would probably be unwise to think of Blake. His Jerusalem may be sung at every BBC prom, his drawings are much admired and his life idolised by many. He did have a long and loving, if childless marriage, but in other respects he was born in the wrong time.

It all looked good at the start. Although he didn't go to school he was apprenticed to an engraver to the Society of Antiquaries, and soon found himself next door, a student at the Royal Academy. But he was a visionary out of step with his time. He was cheated by people like the disreputable Robert Cromek. Blake's couplet 'A petty, sneaking knave I knew. O! Mr Cr—, how do ye do?' *has outlived them both. At one time he was tried for high treason, but was acquitted.*

Most of his life, however hard-working he may have been, he was poor. He was accused of being mad. It is astonishing that he remained witty, even mischievous, up to his death in 1827.

> Piping down the valleys wild,
>   Piping songs of pleasant glee,
> On a cloud I saw a child,
>   And he laughing said to me:
>
> 'Pipe a song about a Lamb!'
>   So I piped with merry cheer.
> 'Piper, pipe that song again;'
>   So I piped: he wept to hear.

'Drop thy pipe, thy happy pipe;
    Sing thy songs of happy cheer!'
So I sung the same again,
    While he wept with joy to hear.

'Piper, sit thee down and write
    In a book that all may read.'
So he vanish'd from my sight;
    And I pluck'd a hollow reed,

And I made a rural pen,
    And I stain'd the water clear,
And I wrote my happy songs
    Every child may joy to hear.

Ben Jonson, born after the death of his father, was a contemporary of Marlowe and Shakespeare, and just as quick as Marlowe to get into a fight.

After Westminster School he worked for his stepfather laying bricks, and then had a short but belligerent spell in the army in Flanders, where he became attracted to the theatre. Back in England, working as an actor and playwright he found himself in prison for sedition, for his part in writing a play called the Isle of Dogs. *The next year he killed a fellow actor in a duel, but escaped execution by pleading benefit of clergy.*

He finally made his mark with a play called Everyman in his Humour, *which also had Shakespeare in the cast. Play followed play, and he was as much loved by his contemporaries, and as loving of them, as anybody at that time. He had many patrons, many friends, and many other poets who sat at his feet in admiration. In 1628 he had a stroke and spent the last nine years of his life bedridden. He was buried in Westminster Abbey, unlike Shakespeare who had been buried twenty one years earlier near the grave of his mother in Holy Trinity.*

Queen and huntress, chaste and fair,
  Now the sun is laid to sleep,
Seated in thy silver chair,
  State in wonted manner keep:
    Hesperus entreats thy light,
    Goddess excellently bright.
Earth, let not thy envious shade
  Dare itself to interpose;

Cynthia's shining orb was made
    Heaven to clear when day did close:
        Bless us then with wishèd sight,
        Goddess excellently bright.

Lay thy bow of pearl apart,
    And thy crystal-shining quiver;
Give unto the flying hart
    Space to breathe, how short soever;
        Thou that mak'st a day of night—
        Goddess excellently bright.

TO AUTUMN

JOHN KEATS

Season of mists and mellow fruitfulness!
  Close bosom-friend of the maturing sun;
Conspiring with him how to load and bless
  With fruit the vines that round the thatch-
      eaves run;
To bend with apples the moss'd cottage-trees,
  And fill all fruit with ripeness to the core;
    To swell the gourd, and plump the hazel shells
  With a sweet kernel; to set budding more,
And still more, later flowers for the bees,
Until they think warm days will never cease,
  For summer has o'er-brimm'd their clammy cells.

Who hath not seen thee oft amid thy store?
  Sometimes whoever seeks abroad may find
Thee sitting careless on a granary floor,
  Thy hair soft-lifted by the winnowing wind;
Or on a half-reap'd furrow sound asleep,
  Drowsed with the fume of poppies, while thy hook
    Spares the next swath and all its twinèd flowers;
And sometimes like a gleaner thou dost keep
  Steady thy laden head across a brook;
  Or by a cider-press, with patient look,
    Thou watchest the last oozings hours by hours.

Where are the songs of Spring? Ay, where are they?
    Think not of them, thou hast thy music too,—
While barrèd clouds bloom the soft-dying day,
    And touch the stubble-plains with rosy hue;
Then in a wailful choir the small gnats mourn
    Among the river sallows, borne aloft
      Or sinking as the light wind lives or dies;
And full-grown lambs loud bleat from hilly bourn;
    Hedge-crickets sing, and now with treble soft
    The redbreast whistles from a garden-croft;
      And gathering swallows twitter in the skies.

Byron was born in 1788 to his father's second wife. He was born with a club foot and a half sister Augusta, each of which had a profound effect on his life and behaviour.

There isn't enough room to give you more than idea about him. By a series of accidents he inherited the title when he was ten, exchanging one kind of poverty for another. He survived Harrow, did well at Cambridge, and because of his good looks and fiery temperament was able to begin a life which his enemies called debauched and his friends viewed with envy. Much the same view was held in England towards his poetry. Critics thought it immoral, which is perhaps why it sold so well all over Europe. Certainly it did manage to bring both him and Murrays, his publishers, occasional very large dollops of money.

Throughout his life there was a series of relationships with different women, whom he treated badly enough to retain their devotion. But his real love seems to have been a romantic ideal of Greece for whose cause to get rid of the Turks he gave freely of his own efforts and his money. When he was twenty one, like Leander, he swam the Hellespont, but unlike Leander he didn't drown. He died instead, aged 36, of a fever he caught in Greece while helping the insurgents prepare to fight the Turks. Neither Westminster Abbey nor St Paul's wanted his body anywhere near their hallowed ground. He was therefore buried near the family seat which he had sold to clear his earlier debts.

She walks in beauty, like the night
　　Of cloudless climes and starry skies;
And all that's best of dark and bright
　　Meet in her aspect and her eyes:
Thus mellow'd to that tender light
　　Which heaven to gaudy day denies.

One shade the more, one ray the less,
　　Had half impair'd the nameless grace
Which waves in every raven tress,
　　Or softly lightens o'er her face;
Where thoughts serenely sweet express
　　How pure, how dear their dwelling-place.

And on that cheek, and o'er that brow,
　　So soft, so calm, yet eloquent,
The smiles that win, the tints that glow,
　　But tell of days in goodness spent,
A mind at peace with all below,
　　A heart whose love is innocent!

Since there's no help, come let us kiss and part—
Nay, I have done, you get no more of me;
And I am glad, yea, glad with all my heart,
That thus so cleanly I myself can free.
Shake hands for ever, cancel all our vows,
And when we meet at any time again,
Be it not seen in either of our brows
That we one jot of former love retain.
Now at the last gasp of Love's latest breath,
When, his pulse failing, Passion speechless lies,
When Faith is kneeling by his bed of death,
And Innocence is closing up his eyes,
   —Now if thou wouldst, when all have given
      him over,
   from death to life thou might'st him yet recover.

Many years ago there was a cartoon in Punch. Two monks in a scriptorium; and the caption is 'I think I've got a hit! Listen! "Sumer is icumen in ..."'

Sumer is icumen in,
    Lhude sing cuccu!
Groweth sed, and bloweth med,
    And springth the wude nu—
    Sing cuccu!

Awe bleteth after lomb,
    Lhouth after calve cu;
Bulluc sterteth, bucke verteth,
    Murie sing cuccu!

Cuccu, cuccu, well singes thu, cuccu:
    Ne swike thu naver nu;
Sing cuccu, nu, sing cuccu,
    Sing cuccu, sing cuccu, nu!

Lhude = loud
Awe = you
Llouth = loweth
Swike = cease

Thomas Carew, like Herrick, Donne, Suckling and others, was one of those who tried to some extent model their work on that of Ben Jonson, whom they idolised. The group was known as the 'Tribe of Ben'. The real quality of Carew's verse tends to have been eclipsed in the firmament of his stellar contemporaries.

Just as it useful to remember that Donne is pronounced to rhyme with bun, in literary cocktail circles you would do well to remember that Carew is pronounced to rhyme with fairy.

The Lady Mary Villiers lies
Under this stone; with weeping eyes
The parents that first gave her birth,
And their sad friends, laid her in earth.
If any of them, Reader, were
Known unto thee, shed a tear;
Or if thyself possess a gem
As dear to thee, as this to them,
Though a stranger to this place,
Bewail in theirs thine own hard case:
    For thou perhaps at thy return
    May'st find thy darling in an urn.

DOVER BEACH
MATTHEW ARNOLD

The sea is calm tonight.
The tide is full, the moon lies fair
Upon the Straits;—on the French coast, the light
Gleams, and is gone; the cliffs of England stand,
Glimmering and vast, out in the tranquil bay.

Come to the window, sweet is the night air!
Only, from the long line of spray
Where the sea meets the moon-blanched land,
Listen! you hear the grating roar
Of pebbles which the waves suck back, and fling,
At their return, up the high strand,
Begin, and cease, and then again begin,
With tremulous cadence slow, and bring
The eternal note of sadness in.

Sophocles long ago
Heard it on the Aegean, and it brought
Into his mind the turbid ebb and flow
Of human misery; we
Find also in the sound a thought,
Hearing it by this distant northern sea.

The sea of faith
Was once, too, at the full, and round earth's shore
Lay like the folds of a bright girdle furled;
But now I only hear

Its melancholy, long, withdrawing roar,
Retreating, to the breath
Of the night-wind, down the vast edges drear
And naked shingles of the world.

Ah, love, let us be true
To one another! for the world which seems
To lie before us like the land of dreams,
So various, so beautiful, so new,
Hath really neither joy, nor love, nor light,
Nor certitude, nor peace, nor help for pain;
And we are here as on a darkling plain
Swept with confused alarms of struggle and flight
Where ignorant armies clash by night.

This poem, written in Latin, was found by Thomas Naogeorgus in a book called Popish Kingdome and Reigne of Antichrist, *which was printed in 1570.*

It was turned into English (they call it 'Englished') by Baranabe Googe (not Barnaby).

Even if you can believe these improbable names in the Oxford Dictionary of Quotations *you may be more comfortable with the fact that it is sometimes attributed to Thomas Forde.*

There is a Lady sweet and kind,
Was never face so pleased my mind;
I did but see her passing by,
And yet I love her till I die.

Her gesture, motion, and her smiles,
Her wit, her voice my heart beguiles,
Beguiles my heart, I know not why,
And yet I love her till I die.

Cupid is wingèd and doth range,
Her country so my love doth change:
But change she earth, or change she sky,
Yet will I love her till I die.

*When he was teaching at Eton in the second half of the
19th century he was known as William Johnson. When he
left teaching he changed his name to Cory, perhaps in the
hope that it would conceal the fact that he also wrote the
Eton Boating Song.*

Fat chance.

They told me, Heraclitus, they told me you were
    dead,
They brought me bitter news to hear and bitter
    tears to shed.
I wept as I remember'd how often you and I
Had tired the sun with talking and sent him down
    the sky.

And now that thou art lying, my dear old Carian
    guest,
A handful of grey ashes, long, long ago at rest,
Still are thy pleasant voices, thy nightingales,
    awake;
For Death, he taketh all away but them he
    cannot take.

Thou still unravish'd bride of quietness,
    Thou foster-child of Silence and slow Time,
Sylvan historian, who canst thus express
    A flowery tale more sweetly than our rhyme:
What leaf-fringed legend haunts about thy shape
    Of deities or mortals, or of both,
        In Tempe or the dales of Arcady?
    What men or gods are these? What maidens loth?
What mad pursuit? What struggle to escape?
        What pipes and timbrels? What wild ecstasy?

Heard melodies are sweet, but those unheard
    Are sweeter; therefore, ye soft pipes, play on;
Not to the sensual ear, but, more endear'd,
    Pipe to the spirit ditties of no tone:
Fair youth, beneath the trees, thou canst not leave
    Thy song, nor ever can those trees be bare;
        Bold Lover, never, never, never canst thou kiss,
Though winning near the goal—yet, do not grieve;
    She cannot fade, though thou hast not thy bliss,
    For ever wilt thou love, and she be fair!

Ah, happy, happy boughs! that cannot shed
    Your leaves, nor ever bid the Spring adieu;
And, happy melodist, unwearièd,
    For ever piping songs for ever new;
More happy love! more happy, happy love!
    For ever warm and still to be enjoy'd,
        For ever panting and for ever young;

All breathing human passion far above,
    That leaves a heart high-sorrowful and cloy'd,
        A burning forehead, and a parching tongue.

Who are these coming to the sacrifice?
    To what green altar, O mysterious priest,
Lead'st thou that heifer lowing at the skies,
    And all her silken flanks with garlands drest?
What little town by river or sea-shore,
    Or mountain-built with peaceful citadel,
        Is emptied of its folk, this pious morn?
And, little town, thy streets for evermore
    Will silent be; and not a soul, to tell
        Why thou are desolate, can e'er return.

O Attic shape! fair attitude! with brede
    Of marble men and maidens overwrought,
With forest branches and the trodden weed;
    Thou, silent form, dost tease us out of thought
As doth eternity: Cold Pastoral!
    When old age shall this generation waste,
        Thou shalt remain, in midst of other woe
    Than ours, a friend of man, to whom thou say'st,
'Beauty is truth, truth beauty,'—that is all
    Ye know on earth, and all ye need to know.

WILLIAM BLAKE

Tyger, Tyger, burning bright
In the forests of the night,
What immortal hand or eye
Could frame thy fearful symmetry?

In what distant deeps or skies
Burnt the fire of thine eyes?
On what wings dare he aspire?
What the hand dare seize the fire?

And what shoulder and what art,
Could twist the sinews of thy heart?
And, when thy heart began to beat,
What dread hand? and what dread feet?

What the hammer? what the chain?
In what furnace was thy brain?
What the anvil? what dread grasp
Dare its deadly terrors clasp?

When the stars threw down their spears,
And water'd heaven with their tears,
Did He smile His work to see?
Did He who made the Lamb make thee?

Tyger, tyger, burning bright
In the forests of the night,
What immortal hand or eye
Dare frame thy fearful symmetry?

John Dowland turned this into a lute song. How could the person who wrote it, or even Dowland, imagine that one day there would be people listening to it on a Walkman as they took their daily exercise!

Weep you no more, sad fountains;
    What need you flow so fast?
Look how the snowy mountains
    Heaven's sun doth gently waste!
But my Sun's heavenly eyes
        View not your weeping,
        That now lies sleeping
Softly, now softly lies
        Sleeping.

Sleep is a reconciling,
    A rest that peace begets;
Doth not the sun rise smiling
    When fair at even he sets?
Rest you then, rest, sad eyes!
        Melt not in weeping,
        While she lies sleeping
Softly, now softly lies
        Sleeping.

What was he doing, the great god Pan,
  Down in the reeds by the river?
Spreading ruin and scattering ban,
Splashing and paddling with hoofs of a goat,
And breaking the golden lilies afloat
  With the dragon-fly on the river.

He tore out a reed, the great god Pan,
  From the deep cool bed of the river;
The limpid water turbidly ran,
And the broken lilies a-dying lay,
And the dragon-fly had fled away,
  Ere he brought it out of the river.

High on the shore sat the great god Pan,
  While turbidly flow'd the river;
And hack'd and hew'd as a great god can
With his hard bleak steel at the patient reed,
Till there was not a sign of the leaf indeed
  To prove it fresh from the river.

He cut it short, did the great god Pan
  (How tall it stood in the river!),
Then drew the pith, like the heart of a man,
Steadily from the outside ring,
And notch'd the poor dry empty thing
  In holes, as he sat by the river.

'This is the way,' laugh'd the great god Pan
    (Laugh'd while he sat by the river),
'The only way, since gods began
to make sweet music, they could succeed.'
Then dropping his mouth to a hole in the reed,
    He blew in power by the river.

Sweet, sweet, sweet, O Pan!
    Piercing sweet by the river!
Blinding sweet, O great god Pan!
The sun on the hill forgot to die,
And the lilies revived, and the dragon-fly
    Came back to dream on the river.

Yet half a beast is the great god Pan,
    To laugh as he sits by the river,
Making a poet out of a man:
The true gods sigh for the cost and pain—
For the reed which grows nevermore again
    As a reed with the reeds of the river.

When I have fears that I may cease to be
Before my pen has glean'd my teeming brain,
Before high-pilèd books, in charact'ry,
Hold like full garners the full-ripen'd grain;
When I behold, upon the night's starr'd face,
Huge cloudy symbols of a high romance,
And feel that I may never live to trace
Their shadows, with the magic hand of chance;
And when I feel, fair creature of an hour!
That I shall never look upon thee more,
Never have relish in the faery power
Of unreflecting love;—then on the shore
    Of the wide world I stand alone, and think,
    Till Love and Fame to nothingness do sink.

UPON JULIA'S CLOTHES
ROBERT HERRICK

Whenas in silks my Julia goes,
Then, then, methinks, how sweetly flows
The liquefaction of her clothes!

Next, when I cast mine eyes and see
That brave vibration each way free,
—O how that glittering taketh me!